AFRICA

CHRONICLES

I

Guy Diffenbaugh, D.D.
Th.D.

Unless noted, all direct scriptural quotations are from the King James Version, KJV of the Bible.

Every attempt has been made by the publisher to secure the appropriate permissions for materials used in this book. If there has been any oversight, we will be happy to rectify the situation and a written request should be made to the publisher.

Africa Chronicles I

ISBN-13: 978-1-948934-03-9

Published by:

Falcon Publishing House, LLC

4251 Monument Road Suite 302

Jacksonville, FL 3222

TABLE OF CONTENTS

Acknowledgements   v

Introduction   vii

Chapter1: Beginnings.   1

Chapter 2: Boots on Ground Togo   9

Chapter 3: East Africa –   41

       Uganda & Kenya

Epilogue.   93

iv

ACKNOWLEDGEMENTS

To God be all the Glory for placing treasure in my earthen vessel and being faithful to pour it out as an offering in His perfect time, a time in my later years, when I wasn't so sure that He remembered my cry to be used for His Kingdom. He is so faithful and good!

To Dr. Nevers Mumba of Zambia, whose passion for his nation lit my fire in the late 1980's when we attended Bible School together at Christ for the Nations.

To Dr. Miezan Niamke of Togo for realizing my call the moment we met and telling me I would come to Togo.

To Apostles Don and Ruthanne Lynch, our fathering leaders, whose leadership and integrity has catapulted us into our calling. They are the best I know at what they do.

To Dr. Lindy Diffenbaugh, my incredible covenant partner, love, intercessor, Mother of our five children, and powerful voice in the Nations. There is no one that could take her place or that I would rather be with.

INTRODUCTION

Several people have encouraged me to record my experiences in Africa. The experiences have been nothing short of amazing, miraculous, and the most fulfilling chapter of my life, so here we go, pen to paper – Chronicles of Africa 1. Book 1 because God is not through with me. Though an older chap, I am, none the less His Ambassador and He tells me there is more. As a retired military officer, I understand authority and following orders. When the King of Kings calls and commissions, the only wise thing to do is to say - "Yes Sir".

Why Africa? Why not Africa? God is about Nations. All Nations are the inheritance of the Son, Jesus Christ (Psalms 2:8). He loves them all and He loves man, whom He created in His image. But Africa is the "Dark Continent" without hope – No more, as God is hovering and Holy Spirit is preparing a massive tsunami of His Glory to restore every bit of greatness He intended for the African people. He had me prophesy this on international television, July 9, 2018, from the daily 7pm-6am revival of "77 Days of Glory" in Kampala, Uganda, which has been going strong since September 18, 2016 with no sign of abating. I expect it to happen. When we speak what Holy Spirit gives us, we are speaking with exousia the Anointing and with the Dunamis power of God behind us, so we should have every expectation and stand firmly in faith believing and knowing that it will come to pass. This is the essence of miracles and we should expect these whenever we speak the Word of God.

I believe the purpose driving this book is to

encourage you to seek Him in the Nations. If you can't physically go, you can go from wherever you are through intercession. There is a people group, region or nation that is waiting for you. It has your name recorded and is awaiting your arrival. Say "Here I am Lord, send me". He will show you and the joy you receive will touch and complete you in areas you can't even imagine.

Will it cost me? You bet it will; everything of value has a steep price. But know this, when you have His vision, He will ensure you have the provision. Answer the King – you will be blessed now and in eternity with money and all the things money can't buy. His Word says so and He will never violate His Word - He watches over it to fulfill it.

Chapter 1

Beginnings

From Glory to Glory

He truly does move us from Glory to Glory when we allow Him. It never seems that way while enduring the trials, which I liken to the blacksmith process of fire and hammering until we became the instrument the Master can use. I can tell you in retrospect that it never ends but you begin to enjoy it as your relationship with Him grows. I've spent a lot of time in the Master's blacksmith shop because I was, perhaps still am, a difficult servant, but I never quit and was convinced I had a destiny and surely He would complete what He started in me and that's a scriptural promise.

I was a career military officer and married an

officer. I was happy and loved what I did. Then I acquired a head injury and couldn't keep up with the responsibilities of a senior officer in the U.S. Army. My wife decided to get out when our first daughter appeared on the scene. I left shortly thereafter and pursued a business opportunity which ended in flames.

We had moved to Dallas, Texas, and one day in 1989, Holy Spirit took me to Christ for the Nations and told me to put my wife in school there. I wasn't sure about this until I told her, and her response was that she had secretly wanted to go there for 15 years. The moment we said yes, all hell came after us. I was run off the highway moving us there and God averted a potential disaster. I was in three automobile accidents within three months, none my fault. Surgery was required and while recuperating, I joined my wife as a student. With the injuries, lack of money, and four young children our marriage was stressed to the breaking point. I also was unaware of the problems the head injury was causing.

My First Taste of Africa

We were in Bible School with students from the nations. I admired the strength and faith of the Africans. Purpose was in everything they did. Then one day Nevers Mumba, a student from Zambia, preached a fiery message and I was sold on Nations. He went on to getting his Nation's President saved. He also went on to become Vice President of Zambia. Today he has a large ministry and is leader of the largest political party in Zambia. I hope to go to Zambia some day and thank him.

Also, during this time, we sang a song from Psalms

2:8 and added "here am I, send me to the Nations". The song became a prayer that would be answered 30 years later. Additionally, although we worked as we went to school, there was never any extra in the finances. The miraculous, for which there is no logical answer, is that two bible students that didn't have two nickels to rub together, paid our tithes and sowed into the Kingdom 6 roofs on international native churches and gave a man of God an automobile as his had holes in the floor and used as much oil as gasoline.

Ironically, the first native church we roofed was in Ivory Coast. Lindy and I had enrolled in an intensive Doctoral program in 2016 and at graduation, I was asked to transport an African from Togo, Miezan Niamke, from the airport. We immediately bonded and a day later he said, "you are coming to Togo". We graduated together, and the enemy came against him and his ministry delaying the process 1 ½ years. Dr. Niamke and his wife were from Ivory Coast, where we first sowed into Africa, but God had sent them to Togo. God gave him victory over his enemies and the door opened.

Church, Perhaps Our Major Stumbling Block

We could not understand why we didn't fit in Churches until we found Freedom House in Jacksonville, Florida. Freedom House, an emerging Regional Ecclesia, brought life to us and we took our share in this body to build the Kingdom. Freedom House is a unique but excellent model. Though small, at perhaps 45 adult members, it is touching 24+ nations in 2018. We work alongside a full complement of 5-fold ministry leaders. The Church is going to shift to the structure Jesus Christ ordained or die. There is not much time left on the prophetic clock. The Ecclesia is the structure Christ gave His apostles and the first century Ecclesia turned the known world upside down with the Gospel. Man thought he could do better and after placing his sin and spin on things we entered the dark ages. The "church", an incorrect translation of the ancient Greek word Ecclesia, means something totally different. I won't go into depth here, as you can read our book Purpose in the King's Call or other excellent resources, but Jesus said He will build His Ecclesia, His form of government on the earth. Our mission is to establish Kingdom Culture.

The Enemy Never Quits

I was scheduled to go to Togo in April 2018 and a month prior I faced death by massive pulmonary embolism. I knew I was on the threshold and told the Lord He could have me, but I really didn't think

I had accomplished my mission. The doctors told me that they could not understand how I survived, and I told them "greater is He who is in me than he who is in the world – I have the Great Physician living inside me".

May 17, 2018, about a month after my hospitalization, I was aboard Air France with destination of Lome, Togo. Glory to God! When I arrived, I discovered that the trip was almost aborted again as Dr. Niamke's wife's father had died. Momma said to move forward with the plan as she only needed to meet with siblings, as her father was a tribal chief and only the new chief was allowed to know where the deceased chief was buried.

I arrived the day before Pentecost.

Dr. Miezan Niamke & Dr. Guy Diffenbaugh

10-30-2016

moving about in their daily routine of survival, sounds, unknown scents, and heat. My room had air conditioning; a blessing of huge proportion. The family gathered, and we were off to church. It was an Assemblies of God church and very much alive. I preached on Pentecost and Holy Spirit. Holy Spirit makes a huge difference when you are in a nation and for me was critical as it was my first and I do not preach often. Truly baptism by fire. After great worship, and Africans know how to worship long, hard, and sincere, it was time.

My Love Affair Begins

As I opened my Bible, took the microphone, and looked at the crowd it happened. I looked into eyes starving for more of God. The African people stole my heart immediately and began a love affair that I will never be able to shake. They so captivated my heart that I knew I would never be the same and would not be able to live too long without my new-found passion. I must have laid hands on just about everyone that morning; it is expected and my joy releasing all God had deposited in me.

Short Pentecost Message for the Youth

We had a meal with the ministry team and went home to rest for the main Pentecost event that evening. My mind, though tired, raced and I wondered if Dr. Lindy would feel the same passion. I prayed that the Lord would captivate her too. I would get my answer soon because she had been invited to her inaugural in Africa, about three weeks after I returned home. I would be going with her as I refuse to send my wife alone and believe that to be wisdom.

Pentecost Evening

We arrived at a large hotel around 10pm. The worship team had been in action for about two hours. This night would end the next morning and my head would hit the pillow at 5:30am. I had never been out so late, or should I say early, even partying before I walked with the Lord. It was an amazing time.

Pentecost Evening Celebration

I preached without notes that evening, completely depending on Holy Spirit. I even prophesied to the nation. I had no idea that we were on national television, which had I known would have probably made me nervous at this point. They all seemed to appreciate the white boy from the USA, but I longed to get the fire of the African. It would come in my next visit to Africa.

My African Family

The Niamkes

The Bishop's Family, my new African Family, and I don't just say this because I really feel like they adopted me. They are amazing in every respect.

There were some cultural as well as language hurdles, but I fell in love with them all.

They had fun trying to feed me as an African. I ate three times my normal intake and it was barely half of what they would consume. Most are slim and fit. It is the diet of fresh natural foods not contaminated with the preservatives and additives that make our culture obese.

The home compound stayed busy as the Bishop and family have a lab in the basement for their oil analysis business with the Port of Lome. They stay busy because Lome is a very busy port for such a small nation and serves surrounding nations. When you look off coast, past the golden sand and palm trees, all you see is ships awaiting their turn.

Ministry is Costly but the King Provides

The Bishop's business fuels his ministry. People

have a misconception that ministers and the church are wealthy, so I intend to diffuse that conception here and now. They are wealthy in that God meets every need in money and what money can't buy. True men and women of God are blessed by the Lord through people, but ministry is costly. Bishop does approximately six large crusades each year. A crusade is an expensive undertaking logistically. I examined the offerings and questioned the Bishop as to how it was possible. The expense was far greater than the offerings received. His response was that God blesses his business and he blesses God's work.

Preparation

The crusade doesn't just happen. Logistical preparation is extensive and African government presents "red tape" just like everywhere else. Bishop has his own equipment but even at that it requires maintenance and preparation. Permits, reconnaissance, coordination, advertisement etc. In other words, it doesn't just happen; there is lots of work involved. This is the daily regimen of preparation. I am telling you about a Reinhard Bonnke style crusade, though instead of a million people we preached to three thousand plus.

Advertisement for the Atakpame, Togo, Crusade

Regardless of size the logistical issues are all there and must be dealt with. Many meetings took place at the house, office, and with ministries that would be attending in the area.

Though the Bishop stepped out on his own under his fathering leader, Apostle Christian Harfouche, USA, we met with the nation's Assembly of God leadership and invited them. In return we were invited to their Bible School graduation in the same town as the crusade. The graduation was large and well attended. It was exciting to see men and women of God that had studied to show themselves approved and many would be the fresh leadership to take the baton and run the race set before us. I also met many of Bishop's teachers and initial mentors. Hot weather for a Florida boy accustomed to air conditioning, but a spectacular time. The Lord gave me a word for one of the graduates and I'm standing in faith to see its manifestation or at least hear of it.

Marking Time

I preached again at another Assembly of God Church in Lome. It was good in every respect, as we were marking time for the crusade. Great

Assembly of God Church in Lome

Worship and loving people,

Bishop took me into the bush to see a church he had built. Anything off the pavement is rough on the body because there is no way for the vehicle to absorb all the shock of bumps and potholes.

Huts in the bush near Lome

It was an adventure and a blessing for the pastor. Additionally, we went to view a tract of land that Bishop plans to obtain and build a large church upon.

Momma is in Ivory Coast attending to matters concerning her late father, a tribal chief. She is missed by all but has the very best driver escorting her. I would trust this man with my life any day. His character, poise, and loyalty are beyond reproach and he is a fashion statement to boot.

Time for a Recon

Four hours of nerve-racking driving into the mountains to Atakpame to do reconnaissance for the crusade beginning May 30, 2018. The town seems to be of medium size. Bishop has rented a sports field with clay ground and some concrete basketball courts. We decide where to set the stage and select accomodations for the team. We meet with local pastors and my interpreter. We return home for more meetings and coordination.

As we travel, the sights are very much the same. Everyone seems to be a merchant. Another observation is that every town has at least one mosque. The Muslim influence grows and thrives because the church has abdicated her responsibilities and the Muslims are quick to fill the void. Bishop tells me that the growth is disturbing.

Back on the Homefront

The women have prepared a meal for the weary travelers. We partake and relax. One of my favorite routines is the several hours of prayer that start at 11pm each night and is perhaps the most timely and rigid event on the calendar. The prayer sessions are powerful and the adult family members all participate. Kingdom business is accomplished in intercession. Yes and amen! I still have not adjusted to African time and perhaps never will, so I just go with the flow.

My Excitement and Anticipation is Growing

My first time in Africa and a real crusade. There are not a lot of these going on because of the difficulty and logistical nightmares. I feel blessed and honored that I will participate in one. Rain is forecast for the entire week. We pray for favorable weather. Bishop tells me that this is nothing new and it has never rained on his crusades. The fact of the matter is that God held the rain back until we had taken the equipment down, loaded, and departed. We arrive to a huge issue in that the towns electrical authority has not dropped a line for us. We pray, and the Supervisor arrives out of nowhere and is unable to understand why power is not there. The Supervisor gets on his cell phone and within 30 minutes we have electrical power. The stage is up as well as the tent where we will be teaching local pastoral leaders. Everything is go.

Evening Comes and it is Time to Preach the Glorious Gospel

The crowd had gathered and been worshipping for several hours. We arrive about 10pm. Bishop preaches the first night. We have an altar call for salvation and receive several dozen from amongst 2500 + of the attendees. Then we have a call for prayer and healing. The altar is flooded. One of the first forward is a lame woman whom I will never forget. The Lord told me that she was a progressive miracle. She understood and her faith resonated. Many were healed and set free. The demonic was my largest surprise. The demonic in Togo is extremely strong. Some were quickly set free, but several had married spirits under the water and these demons didn't want to leave their victims. It took three men to contain some of the women and then the battle began. Some of these took as many as ten minutes to be set free as they thrashed about with eyes rolling to the back of their head. I had never heard of this demonic marriage under water but know the spirit world is more real than the natural and upon study I read many accounts of this activity, especially in west Africa.

Crusade Day 2

Around 10am we go to the tent to teach pastoral leadership. My focus is Kingdom which seemed to be a practically new teaching. They soaked it up and I made sure that each understood that I was not trying to be divisive, rather trying to unify the leadership to accomplish the purpose of God for which they were called in this hour. During this time, I heard the Muslim call to prayer which has always been a demonic sound to me. I looked out the tent in daylight and saw a mosque on the hill about 50 yards behind the stage. I asked God to silence the call to prayer issuing forth from the mosque. God is good and gave us all that we asked for. I never heard the call to prayer again. We finished around 2pm and went to the hotel for rest. We go again at 10pm and it is my turn to preach. I preached a basic salvation message and had an altar call. I can't understand why it took them so long to present, but they began to come.

Dr. Guy preaching on Day 2

The numbers don't make sense, several dozen from amongst 3000+. When the call for healing comes, we see just how many have back-slidden and have opened themselves to the demonic. They want to be set free, with some retaining the healing and growing strong while others boost in faith wains and the enemy finds a weak point to enter into their destruction. It is not a uniquely African problem, rather is worldwide. I will state that an African sold out to Jesus Christ is a powerful force against the kingdom of darkness.

My first to come forward was the lame woman, using a staff to steady herself as she dragged one leg. It seemed as if it took her forever to reach me. I prayed with her and told her that Jesus would heal her but that it would be a progressive miracle requiring her faith.

The following night she dragged the lame leg for perhaps 20 yards and a seeming eternity to the point where I sat with the clergy and sat at my feet. This disturbed some of the ministers and they came to escort her away. I asked to minister to her. I asked her if she believed in Jesus and if she believed He was able to heal her. She said yes, so I laid hands on her and she went back to where

she had come from at a gait three times as fast.

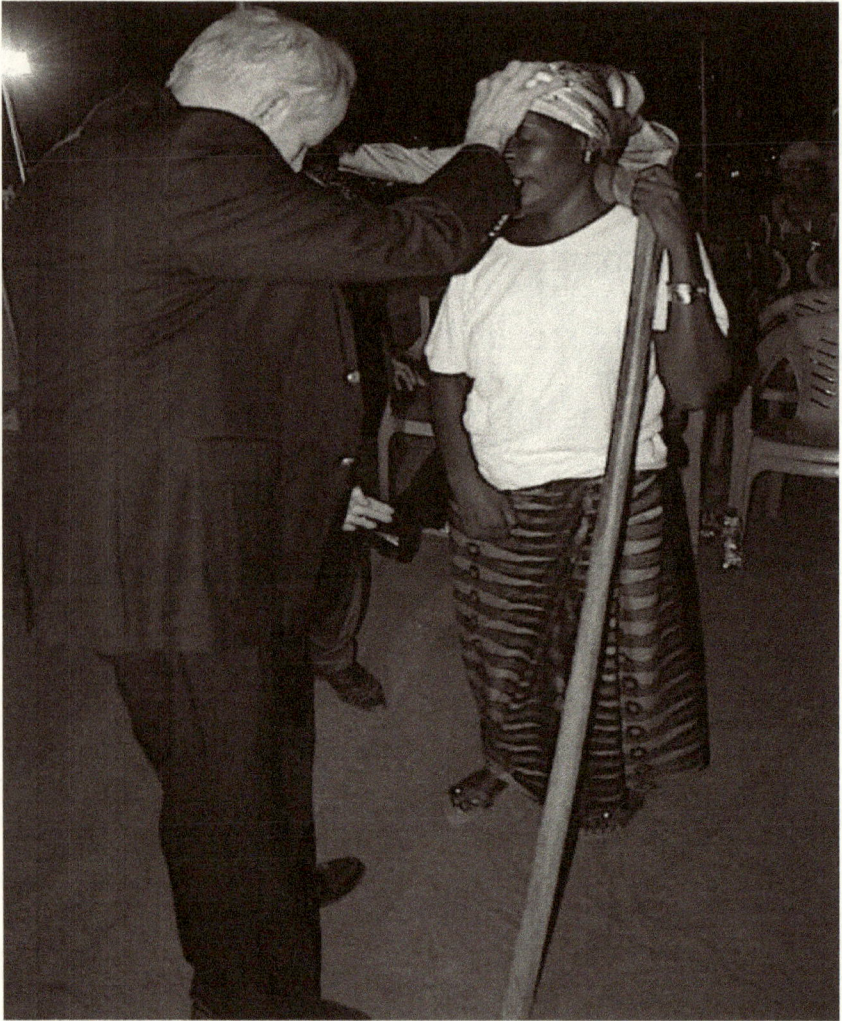

The Lame Lady Receiving Healing

The demonstrative demons continued to oppose and disrupt but began to lessen. I was attacked when I tried to get out of bed the next day. My head was spinning and I could not stand so I laid back down and rebuked the attack. About fifteen minutes later I was ok and ready to go. Thus, began day three.

Crusade Day 3

I am tired from the previous day and the demonic assault, but some breakfast and coffee invigorated me and I was ready to teach pastors. I taught on the age old but forgotten concept of kingdom and Ecclesia. I drilled deep and made sure all understood as I did not want their leadership trying to invalidate or pronounce us as heretics. I believe they finally got it. My new friend, Charles, from Ghana, was a big help. Suddenly, the Bishop said we must leave. It turns out that he was under the same attack I had experienced. He asked me if I could drive and I really had no choice. It was nerve racking, but we made it back to the hotel.

Evening comes and Momma Niamke has joined us. Her strength and presence are felt. Bishop preaches tonight, and it is excellent. The crowd has grown from word of mouth and we have a powerful evening. The presence and power of the Almighty is with us and Holy Spirit ministers the miraculous through us setting the captive free. Ministry to the people is amazing. I prayed and laid hands on so many that my arm ached. It is very fulfilling to pour out the Anointing and see the Lord perform the miraculous in these hungry lives. These are truly days that I will never forget, a culmination of dreams.

Ministering in Africa drains you completely and the pillow feels amazing. It is very fulfilling and a rare privilege to preach and minister in a crusade. God is so good and so faithful. After so many years of transformation, much of the delay being me, He thrusted me and trusted me in the nations. Is He speaking to you, as there can be no higher call than taking the Glorious Gospel to the Nations. There is no greater high or revelation of purpose.

Crusade Day 4

The final day arrives. There is no training and we get much needed rest. I was able to pray and get into the word. I so much wanted to be on target this final evening.

I don't recall what I preached but it was Holy Spirit given at the last minute, which has become my favorite way to preach. I had been praying that I could preach with the power of the African. My message was good, but the powerful African delivery would come about a month later on my second time of ministry in East Africa. We ministered to the people and it was over. I will never forget my first crusade and look forward doing this again in the near future.

Dr. Guy Preaching 4th Night

Crusade Day 5

Each of us went to preach at Sunday services in the area. I have a congregation of about thirty. I delivered the message Holy Spirit gave me and prayed for everyone. It is expected in Africa that the Evangel lay hands on all that want prayer. Though miracles presented, I discovered that many issues, especially with the children, could be solved by medication and the drinking of good water.

When finished I went outside and sat on a bench under a shade tree. While speaking with the Lord and expressing my gratitude for all He had done through us, a light rain began to fall. Perfect timing — the Lord had held back the predicted rain for the length of the crusade and allowed the team to disassemble the equipment and get out before the rain. He is so good and always faithful. He withheld the rain, stopped the Muslim call to prayer, showed up in power and provided for us all. Glory to the living God.

Back to Lome

Four hours of hectic driving and we are at Bishop's home. The remainder of my stay in West Africa will be rest and further bonding with my amazing new African family. I am really exhausted from pouring out all I had for God's people.

Bishop says, "Do you think Dr. Lindy can handle the demonic?" I replied that she is an Intercessor and loves removing the darkness. I suggested we ask her and proceeded to call her. I asked the question and her reply was "the question should be – can the demons handle me?" Bishop liked the response and said: "you will bring Momma to Togo next year and I have plans for her in Togo, Ivory Coast, and Ghana."

The remainder of my stay was everyday family interaction and meeting the numerous guests that visit the Bishop. Bishop stays busy with his business, family and all those that seek his wisdom and counsel.

All good things must temporarily end

The African people captured my heart and when my departure time arrived, I found myself sad to leave my new family and friends. I was really missing Dr. Lindy, my family, dogs, and friends, but the departure was hard. (Dogs are not important to Africans and I'm quite sure they have no concept of the love for these creatures in the USA and other countries).

Crusade Team Musicians bid me farewell

God has given me a love affair with these people and I'm sure He will let me return a few more times before my eternal reward. My Fathering Leader, Apostle Don Lynch, says I was born for this. I now know this and there will always be a restlessness and desire to go. There is nothing more rewarding and fulfilling than preaching the Glorious Gospel in the Nations.

God Bless the USA

Most Americans have no concept of how blessed they are. If only our country could understand this, we would be strong like we were in the early years of the Republic. Though I'm certain our moral and spiritual decay is a stench in His nostrils, as is our repudiation for the Son He sacrificed on our behalf, I believe God is exceptionally merciful to us because we provide hope and life-giving substance to the world, as well as sending Believers into the nations.

It was nice to touch US soil and be with my loved ones. I am excited that I get to return in three weeks with my amazing wife, Dr. Lindy. There is no one I would rather be with than this beautiful dynamo of power. I am praying that Africa will steal her heart too.

Chapter 3

East Africa: Uganda and Kenya

Barely over jet lag, several weeks later on July 4, 2018, we spend the night in Fort Lauderdale, FL for an early morning flight to Newark-Dubai-Entebbe. Africa is a long and tiring jet ride but with Kingdom DNA and the Gospel in your heart, purpose is a treasure far more valuable than any amount momentary pain or inconvenience. This distance to Uganda is about 2,200 miles farther than Lome, Togo, making it a very long time to be riding an airplane. We arrive July 6th and hit the ground running.

Dr. Lindy was invited to speak at a women's conference with some others from the USA. Apostle Don Lynch said we would face some problems but the good would more than outweigh the bad. I went with her as I would never send my wife alone to be with people we didn't know, and it was her first time to Africa. We would find things just as the Apostle said but would have a glorious trip with fulfilment of purpose and establishment of special contacts to covenant and partner with for ministry. A tip from the school of hard knocks; minister in the nations with leaders you have worked with. Lindy was one of five invited from the USA and two dropped out, so I became an active part of the team.

The invitation was from Mugisa Elijah of Fort Portal, Uganda. Mugisa has preached the Gospel since he was twelve years old and is the right-hand man of Jimmy Katuramu, Bishop of the United Pentecostal Churches International of Uganda. Mugisa is also the lead pastor of a government organization called RUNEDI or Rural Needy Development Initiative. Pastor Mugisa had a vision and saw Dr. Lindy's name in neon lighting on a telephone pole. He searched the internet until he found her and the two communicated for months and shortly before my departure for Togo, she received the invitation to minister in Uganda and Kenya.

Elijah's get new shoes

Diffenbaugh's get new clothes

We have a busy schedule with ministry almost nonstop and a whole lot of travel. The first ministry will be the Women's Conference in Kampala at the Double Anointing International Ministries Church led by Pastor Anthony Kamanyl.

When I got my turn, I preached with the African fire that had been my prayer. **Holy Spirit led me to prophesy to Africa. I declared that "Africa was no longer to be the dark continent and that God has not forgotten these people groups and that He is hovering and desires to pour out immeasurable blessing and revival as Holy Spirit comes like a tsunami bringing life to pour into your nations and to the world."** Holy Spirit would have me give this everywhere I went, and I am getting feedback even today that many have taken this to heart and are standing in faith believing and expecting His hand to move Africa out of bondage.

Bishop Guy praying for mother and child

We preached the Gospel and experienced the miraculous Dunamis power of Almighty God.

We all made contributions to prepare food for the people. Some had walked for miles and slept on the dirt floor of the church.

The Breakout Sessions

On the way to the Breakout session Dr. Lindy asks where the fire came from, as she had never seen that in me. I explained that I had asked the Lord for African fire and He provided. We had an excellent session with the women. Our problems are so miniscule to theirs. Many had HIV or AIDS and the husbands usually left them and the children. Many of the husbands had multiple partners. Many wives wanted to go to church but were not allowed or had no way of getting to the church. The problems are self-perpetuating, and the devil is not having to work very hard to steal, kill, and destroy these people. The hope these ladies have is solely the Lord. The government can't take care of all these issues. The Church must rise and be the Church. Growth of Islam is fast becoming an issue, and many have taken on Muslim men because the Mosques provide what the government and Church can't or won't. Another issue we discovered and was universally true was lack of Bibles. Many of these women simply could not afford them. The team purchased some Bibles, but the need was beyond our resources. Dr. Lindy and I decided that Bibles for Africa would be a priority in how we would help these people. I will tell you later in this volume about the start of our effort in this area.

We also want to do something to educate the men and women in ministry.

Bp. Guy and Dr. Lindy, Breakout session with the Women and Pastor's Wife Interpreting

After a great session, we have our first Ugandan meal. Dr. Lindy decides to live on the fresh fruit and occasionally some beans. The standard meal consists of a small amount of chicken, goat, or beef, lots of rice, beans, cooked mashed bananas, millet and fresh fruit. It is actually very healthy because it is fresh with no preservatives or sugar. Most Africans are lean though they eat in one setting what would be three meals for me.

Dr. Lindy's next horror is there are few toilets, and these are mostly found in some hotels. The Africans use a rectangular hole in the floor approximately 12x6 inches.

We preach again after the meal then to the hotel. As in Togo nothing runs on a strict schedule as Africa pays no attention to time. It does no good to get frustrated as an American or European would. The African will respond "this is Africa".

Pastor's wife Prossy and son

In East Africa I am referred to as Bishop or Papa and Lindy as Dr. or Mama. Africans are respectful, humble, and loving.

We bonded well with everyone. The Pastors

Kamanyl, Anthony and Prossy, would later ask Dr. Lindy and myself to be their fathering or spiritual leaders. They are a young power couple loved by all and their impact in the Kingdom will grow.

We ministered to their people and guests for two and a half days. It was hard to leave but we will see them again. We would shop for some Bibles printed in the various languages of places we would visit, then to John Mulinde's Prayer Mountain in Kampala.

Dr. Lindy at John Mulinde's Prayer Mountain in Kampala

It was dark when we arrived, but we prayed and spoke the word of the Lord into the nation/nations. John Mulinde is World Overseer of Global Trumpet Ministries and a man of prayer. With a heart to see Africa set free from deception and oppression, he established a prayer mountain where many come for days or weeks of intercession, living in tents and caves. This was an important stop for Dr. Lindy as she is an Intercessor dedicated to prayer and worship and had read Mulinde's books. She will preach a message stimulated from his book Prayer Altars.

On the way to the hotel we visited another spiritual activity called 77 Days of Glory. Pastor Robert and Jessica Kayanja started this work of God on the 18th of September 2016 and the revival crusade is daily from 7pm to 6am. Many conversions and miracles have happened in this

Crusade. The stage is surrounded with some of the many crutches, wheel chairs, and Muslim caps of those healed and set free. It is estimated that they have touched well over a hundred million lives for Christ through social media, international television, and live visits. As international guests we are seated at the front and at a point in the service we will introduce ourselves on international television. Dr. Lindy is exhausted and heads for the van prior to the introduction of the international visitors. When the International visitors were introduced, Holy Spirit led me to repeat my prophesy about Africa, which several international friends told me they viewed. Pastor Kayanja prayed for me and handed me an envelope of money for our ministry. The gift was God ordained as He knew we would need the money for expenses we had not anticipated.

The revival crusade is still running strong as I pen these chronicles. Glory to God!

77 Days of Glory Revival Crusade – Kampala

Welcome sleep, good breakfast and fellowship and we are off to Mugisa's home in Fort Portal on

July 10th with a short stop to meet Dr. Richard, who has the King's ear as well as that of the Prime Minister. Dr. Richard shares my exact thoughts as to how Uganda's issues can be solved. In simplistic terms it is give a person a fish and he is hungry the next day – give him a fishing pole and the problem is solved. Uganda depends heavily on outside help when they really have all the resources they need to be self-sufficient at some point. They need God, medicine, and education. I salute philanthropists Bill and Melinda Gates for the massive amount of medicine they have sent to Africa to combat the HIV/AIDS problem.

Dr. Richard and I agree as he pledges his support and encouragement for any initiative we desire for Uganda and will see us in a week when he returns from medical meetings in the United Kingdom.

We begin our long drive to Fort Portal. The country

is beautiful and the weather delightful. Each town has the small merchants selling their goods. Fresh fruit is everywhere and copious amounts of green bananas that I believe are sort of like plantain. The stalks of the green bananas are several inches in diameter and laden with this staple of the African diet. Most of the yellow ready to eat bananas are small, fresh, sweet, and very tasty. As in Togo, motor bikes or "moto" are everywhere. Our driver, William, is skilled and always alert to our safety. He would later, in Kagadi, give his life to the Lord based upon the witness of the ministry team from USA. He would also change his ways and pledge to marry the woman he lived with.

We arrive in the dark and awaken to what is considered the most beautiful area of Uganda with lush green rolling hills. Fort Portal has a lot of British history and residents. This part of western

Uganda is full of tea plantations. The British built a fort here between 1891-1893. It is also the home of the youngest Ugandan Kingdom of Tooro and the youngest monarch to ever assume a throne at four years old in 1995. We were supposed to meet the King, but our ministry schedule did not match his schedule.

Kamwenge

We are going to Kamwenge, southeast of Fort Portal. The young pastor is doing a splendid work there. We went through the forest where all African animals can be seen. We do see baboons which come up to our van. The ride is long with some paved road and clay roads full of potholes that beat you unmercifully. The van is an exceptional vehicle as it takes a severe beating from our travels. Our bodies take a beating also and at our age I am grateful for our military life and that we have worked to remain fit. We are in Kamwenge for two days. When it was my turn to preach the Lord tells me to have an old retired pastor pray for me. I felt the power of God flow through me as never before and it took me a few minutes to be able to stand. Dr. Lindy tells me that she felt the power on the other side of the room. We preached the word and as is African custom laid hands on all.

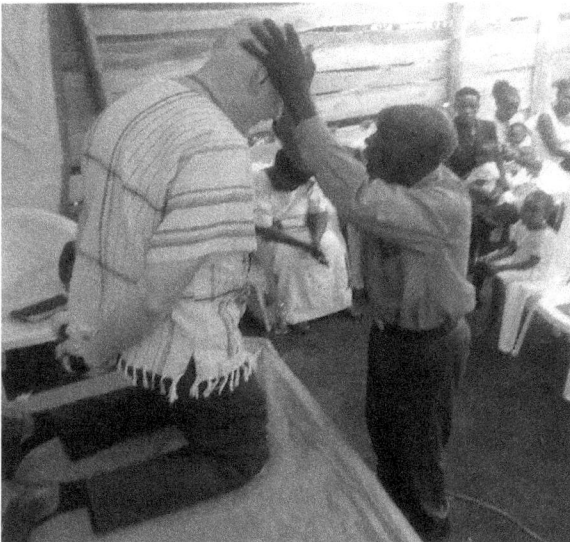

The elderly Man of God prays for me

Bishop Guy brings the Word

Dr. Lindy delivers the Word

After the team's messages, we broke into groups. I had the pastors, Dr. Lindy the women, Coleen the children and Josh the youth. We fielded questions and suggested possible ways to improve the situations. Africans are so gracious.

The morning of July 13 we return to Fort Portal visit Pastor Masiko Blessing's Church and the prison where he ministers, as well as addressing his Church and breaking bread with him and the people. He has a strong ministry with a lot on his plate. Dr. Lindy and I will preach here Sunday while the others go to another church. Afterwards we will all have a meal with Pastor Blessing and visit a honey producing business in the middle of nowhere. Honey is mentioned 61 times in scripture such as in Proverbs 24:13 where it says to eat honey as it is good. Raw honey is good for you and aids in dreaming if taken before bedtime.

Dr. Lindy gives a message on Prayer

Next, we visited an orphanage, the RUNEDI supports, containing many orphans whose parents lost their lives in the violence of the Congo or to AIDS. I don't think we can really imagine the suffering these children have endured in their young lives. If not for the mercy of God and the Church these precious children would not exist.

Dr. Lindy speaks to the Orphanage

Tomorrow we meet Bishop Jimmy Katuramu at his school, meet with RUNEDI personnel and attend an African wedding in which Pastor Mugisa's wife, Evelyn, is participating as matron of honor. But rest is needed from a very busy day ending in the witness of suffering children.

Dr. Lindy, Bp. Jimmy Katuramu, & Bp. Guy

Bishop Jimmy's School

RUNEDI operates on a lean budget, far less than the need, but does excellent work with the communities it serves. We experience some of the initiatives to assist the populace in becoming self-supporting. We plan for our travel to Kasese on the morrow and attend the afternoon wedding feast. Africans do these events with excellence and flair.

We did not arrive in time for the elaborate introduction ceremony, but Dr. Richard has invited us to one and I will elaborate when that sequence of events happens. We arrived at the time of the reception and presentation of gifts.

The Wedding Party

Travel to Kasese

Kasese is a rough ride of about three hours on roads that will jar your teeth out. On these roads the red clay dust begins to work on your sinus and turns light colored garments orange. Dr. Lindy has black shoes with black ribbons that now have a permanent orange tint. This congregation of the Bunyamurwa Full Gospel Church, led by Pastor Jimmy Byamuka, is high up in the Rwenzori Mountains. Claudius Ptolemy, the Greco-Roman mathematician, astronomer and father of geography, called the Rwenzori range the Mountains of the Moon because of their height. The highest one is 5109 meters in elevation which is 16,762 feet. I am guessing that we were up about 12,000 feet. The mountains separate Uganda from the Republic of the Congo. It is stunningly beautiful.

The Kasese Church in Worship

Bishop Guy's message to the Saints at Kasese

Some of these people had never seen a white

person. Dr. Lindy followed me and preached her altars message which was very Anointed. The pastor would call us the next day to report that his people went home and burned their idols and many had experienced miracles.

Bishop Guy & Dr. Lindy in Kasese

We poured out all we had and couldn't wait to get some sleep after 3 more hours of rough ride back to Fort Portal.

North to Kagadi

Kagade is another long hard ride on roads that beat you. We are off to Kagadi which is not far removed from canabalism and near the home of a man claiming to be the Messiah and known for the miraculous. He had a large following requiring government intervention. We arrive to a joyous group at United Pentecostal Church under leadership of Pastor Innocent Kwaringa. The Church members have a parade through the town. This is the time our driver, William, gives his life to Jesus. Two days of powerful ministry.

Dr. Lindy Deliver the Word in Kagadi

Dr. Lindy preached and taught about Intercession as well as altars. We let the youngsters do the evening crusade. We expected and witnessed miracles, to include the driver, William's salvation. This was a very needy group with the largest group of saints without Bibles. They were so hungry for a Bible of their own that they nearly fought to grab one. This is where Dr. Lindy and I decided to make

Bibles for Africa a priority. We asked for a show of hands of those who didn't own a Bible and the picture is self-explanatory.

Those without Bibles at the Pentecostal Church, Kagadi

On the return trip to Fort Portal, I was quickened to look behind us and see that the tailgate was open. We had lost luggage of which two pieces were our small bags containing passports and other valuables. William secured the hatch and we back tracked for miles recovering all. One bag was being secured to a young man's moto as we drove up. The Lord was looking out for us and continued His goodness and favor at all times. The Lord averted a potentially expensive loss of time and money.

Glory to Him who alone is worthy!

Miraculous Recovery of our Ejected Luggage

Back to Fort Portal with travel to Kenya on tap for tomorrow.

Fort Portal to Kampala to Busia border crossing to Luanda Town Kenya

It was as a long trip and adventure. We did break it up with an overnight stay in Kampala and somehow it took all of the following day and way into the evening to arrive. The faithful Kenyans were waiting for us at the World Christian Ministry Church and fired up to get with the program. Being it was 10pm we said it would have to wait until the morning. I immediately liked the Kenyans and could feel the depth of their sincerity and conviction. The heathen are a different story partying all night. The next day we changed hotels and faced much the same but no loud band. We bonded well with Archbishop Godfrey and other

Bishops, Pastors, and people of God.

Bishop Guy with Archbishop and Host Bishop

The Archbishop was so loving and gracious. After

hearing Dr. Lindy and I preach, he told us we could

not have learned the message from school or man but said it was straight from God. Not sure what we preached that was so anointed, but we do place expectation on the anointing that comes upon when Holy Spirit moves. Anyway, we had to promise that we would return. We have committed to a week in March 2019 at the border church in Busia. Apostle Javan Outlah Masimba has organized a conference and asked us to be the main speakers. He attests to seeing sparks come out of my mouth which is testimony to me that God gave me a good dose of the African fire I had pleaded for.

Dr. Lindy loving on a Ugandan baby girl

Kampala for the night headed again to Fort Portal

After a good rest we did some sightseeing and shopping in Kampala before going back to Fort Portal, a good five-hour drive. We have been invited by Dr. Richard to attend an African

Introduction. This is a festive occasion where the bride's parents and friends sit in a large tent across from the groom's parents and friends. There is an elaborate procedure with entertainment and revelry and the negotiations are made where the groom's family must pay the brides. It involves money and livestock and the amount depends much on the family wealth. I don't know how much money changed hands, but the bride's family got money and six cows. The main men involved, and any visiting male dignitaries were required to wear a special garment. After the negotiations the couple marries, there is dancing and a meal.

Entertainment

Bishop Guy and Dr. Richard in Ceremonial Garments

The following day we visit a restaurant to decide for a special meal. I had been noticing that some people looked at me strange and now I find out why. On the counter is a picture of my double. The deceased man was a famous Missionary to Uganda. I sent the picture to friends and they thought it was me.

Famous Papa to Uganda from the UK

Winding Down a Great Time of Ministry

It is 29 July and time to preposition in Kampala for our flight home. We awaken the next morning to a tragic phone call that our youngest son has died. Kind of in shock we take the long flights home.

Sacrifice is Painful

We sowed into Eternity the most precious seed a parent can sow. He is a man of God, now with his Master, and his life a testimony to the same.

Though we think of Jonathan daily, Dr. Lindy and I have stood strong as a witness to our family and our God. I don't know if we could have averted the loss if we had been home, as opposed to doing His will in the nations, but we can you assure that our passion now runs even deeper and hotter than ever before.

In lieu of flowers we started a memorial in

Jonathan's name to begin providing Bibles to Africa.

JONATHAN PAUL DIFFENBAUGH

8/16/1997-7/29/2018

Bibles to Double Anointing Church in Kampala, Uganda

Bibles for Busia Church in Kenya

Bibles for Luanda Kisumu in Kenya

Bibles for Nairobi Church, Kenya

Bible distribution in Fort Portal, Uganda

Receipt of Bibles in Fort Portal, Uganda

We speak blessings on all those who sowed into this good ground. The seed you sowed will return to you multiplied and that is a Biblical promise.

Epilogue

I sincerely hope you have enjoyed my Chronicles of Africa and that perhaps it has inspired you to venture out into the deep. As I said we are all called to nations, even if it is through intercession alone. It is the high calling and the foremost priority of God. When we begin to think and act like our Creator it moves His hand. He will move Heaven and Earth to accomplish His will through you. Although the Godhead could exist without us, that is not His desire. Just ponder the fact that you are created in His image with precious promises that He was willing to sacrifice His Son for, that we might have life and life abundantly.

Our mandate is to go and make disciples. We now receive more requests than we can fulfill. We will be going to Africa again in early of 2019. Can there be anything more important than sharing the salvation and love of God? I think not.

COME THY KINGDOM - WILL OF GOD HAPPEN, on Earth as it is in Heaven.

Be Glorified in our lives and the Nations! Yes, and Amen.

www.ingramcontent.com/pod-product-compliance
Lightning Source LLC
Chambersburg PA
CBHW021205020426
42331CB00003B/208